COUNTRIES OF THE WORLD

SWEDEN

LEIF SCHACK-NIELSEN

☑®

Facts On File, Inc.

Sweden

Copyright © 2006 by Evans Brothers Limited

All rights reserved. No part of this book may be reproduced or utilized in any form or by any means, electronic or mechanical, including photocopying, recording, or by any information storage or retrieval systems, without permission in writing from the publisher. For information contact:

Facts On File, Inc.
132 West 31st Street
New York NY 10001

Library of Congress Cataloging-in-Publication Data
Schack-Nielsen, Leif, 1948–
Sweden / Leif Schack-Nielsen.
  p. cm.— (Countries of the world)
Includes bibliographical references and index.
 ISBN 0-8160-6012-6
1. Sweden—Description and travel—Juvenile literature. I. Title.
II. Countries of the world (Facts On File, Inc.)
 DL619.5.S33 2005
948.5—dc22   2005052882

Facts On File books are available at special discounts when purchased in bulk quantities for businesses, associations, institutions, or sales promotions. Please call our Special Sales Department in New York at (212) 967-8800 or (800) 322-8755.

You can find Facts On File on the World Wide Web at http://www.factsonfile.com.

Printed in China by Leo Paper Products Ltd.

10 9 8 7 6 5 4 3 2 1

Editor: Susie Brooks
Designer: Jane Hawkins
Map artwork: Peter Bull
Charts and graphs: Encompass Graphics Ltd.

Photograph acknowledgments
All by Leif Schack-Nielsen except: 11 top, 41 bottom (Pascal le Segretain, Getty Images); 16 left (Topfoto.co.uk); 18 (Philippe Henri, Still Pictures); 39 top, 40 (Sven Nackstrand/AFP, Getty Images); 46 bottom (Jason Lindsey/Photographers Direct, Perceptive Visions).

First published by Evans Brothers Limited,
2A Portman Mansions, Chiltern Street,
London W1U 6NR, United Kingdom.

This edition published under license from Evans Brothers Limited. All rights reserved.

Endpapers (front): Seventeenth-century buildings surround Stortorget, the main square in the old center of Stockholm.
Title page: Walkers in the mountainous area of Idre, close to Sweden's border with Norway.
Imprint and Contents page: Farmland in the southern province of Skåne.
Endpapers (back): Scenery of the *skärgård* islands near Orust on the northwest coast of Sweden.

CONTENTS

The Swedish flag became official in 1906, but it has been used since the sixteenth century. The cross symbolizes Christianity, and the colors are those of the fourteenth-century shield of state.

Coniferous forests, studded with lakes, cover much of Sweden's landscape.

The Kingdom of Sweden lies in northern Europe. It is one of the five Scandinavian countries, which also include Norway, Denmark, Finland and Iceland. Sweden has the largest population of the five, but also the biggest land area, so many parts of the country are sparsely inhabited. Sweden is a modern, highly industrialized nation, and one of the richest in the world.

COUNTIES AND TRANSPORT

Main road
Railroad
International airport
County divisions

UNDERSTANDING SWEDEN'S GEOGRAPHY

Geographical descriptions of Sweden can be confusing. The country is divided into 21 counties, or *län* in Swedish. These are administrative regions that were introduced in 1634. Before that, the land was split into 25 provinces (*landskap*) – and these are still acknowledged today. Some of the counties correspond to similarly named provinces – for example Skåne in the south. Others are different – Lappland, for example, is a province that overlaps several differently named counties in the north. Most Swedes mention their province rather than their county when they talk about their homes.

There are visible contrasts between the different parts of Sweden, not only in its landscapes but also in people's traditions. As a result, residents in the outlying provinces sometimes feel detached from the capital, Stockholm. Nevertheless, Swedes stick firmly together as one nation.

People shopping in the center of Sweden's capital, Stockholm.

SWEDISH RULE

Sweden is a constitutional monarchy. This means that the country has a king and the title is inherited, but the king has only symbolic power. The country is governed by a parliament (*Riksdagen*) which is appointed through a general election every four years. The prime minister is chosen by the 349 members of parliament, and he or she appoints a cabinet. The foremost political party has for many years been the Social Democratic Party. Under this leadership, Sweden has gathered strength in welfare and democracy.

Every county (*län*) has its own administration selected by the government, but there is also an area council with representatives elected locally. Each county is divided into several municipalities, each with its own council and administration.

PROVINCES

KEY DATA

Official Name:	Kingdom of Sweden
Area:	449,964km^2
Population:	9,002,500 (2004)
Capital City:	Stockholm
Currency:	Swedish krona (SEK)
GDP Per Capita:	US$26,750*
Highest Point:	Kebnekaise (2,111m)
Exchange Rate:	US$1 = 7.47 kronor
	£1 = 13.54 kronor

*(2003) Calculated on Purchasing Power Parity basis
Source: *CIA World Factbook; World Bank*

SWEDEN'S HISTORY

Archaeological findings from all over Sweden show that the land has been populated for several thousand years. During the Iron Age (c. 500 B.C.–A.D. 800) and the Viking era (A.D. 800–1050), the area around present-day Stockholm became a center of commerce and power. One of the biggest and busiest Viking towns was Birka at Lake Mälaren. Here, goods such as fur from Russia were traded with items including jewelry and weapons from northern and central Europe.

ESTABLISHING A KINGDOM

During Viking times, the Swedish state began to take shape. The land gradually changed from a collection of small chiefdoms, each with its own king, to a unified country. The Kingdom of Sweden seems to have been established by the twelfth century.

In 1389, Norway, Denmark and Sweden were brought together under one king – a Dane. The Swedes felt dominated by this union, and in 1523 they rebelled. As a result the Swedish nobleman Gustav Vasa was elected king of Sweden. In subsequent years, Sweden became one of the most powerful countries in Europe, also governing what is now Finland, some of the Baltic States and parts of northern Germany. But this position did not last for long.

In 1809, Sweden lost Finland – a major part of its territory – to Russia in the Napoleonic Wars. In an attempt to compensate for the lost area, Sweden forged a union with Norway in 1814. But the Norwegians wanted their own independent country, so the union was dissolved in 1905. Since that time Sweden has had no territorial problems or changes.

SWEDISH NEUTRALITY

During both the First and Second World Wars, Sweden was one of the few European nations that remained neutral. Swedes took no part in the fighting, and there were no foreign troops in the country. This meant that Sweden saved a lot of money and was spared considerable suffering, so development after the Second World War was much quicker than in most European countries.

INTERNATIONAL COOPERATION

Sweden is traditionally closely connected to the other Nordic countries. In 1952, Sweden, Denmark, Norway, Finland, Iceland, Greenland, the Faroe Islands and the Åland Islands formed

Ales Stenar in the province of Skåne is a mysterious series of rocks, laid out in the shape of a massive ship. It was created during the Iron Age, around 1,400 years ago.

People celebrate Sweden's decision to keep its own currency, after a clear majority of Swedes voted against the euro in a national referendum.

the different nations meet regularly to discuss common issues. One outcome of this collaboration is a Nordic Passport Union, which allows citizens of the Nordic countries to travel to the other Nordic countries without a passport. Also, Nordic citizens may live, work and study as they wish within these countries.

In 1995, Sweden became a member of the European Union. However, like Denmark and Norway, the country has so far opted out of European monetary union. The currency in Sweden is still the Swedish krona, as opposed to the European euro.

Because of its neutrality, Sweden never joined NATO. However, the Swedes still cooperate militarily with other nations.

the Nordic Council – an organization that enables the countries to cooperate in the areas of culture, education, business, human rights, the environment, and the development of democracy and social security.

Sweden also works together with its neighboring countries through the Nordic Council of Ministers, where politicians from

The ship *Vasa*, built for the Swedish king in 1628, was found on the bottom of Stockholm's harbor. Now on show in a multilevel museum, it attracts visitors from around the world.

LANDSCAPE AND CLIMATE

Lake Vänern is the biggest of Sweden's Great Lakes.

Sweden is the largest of the Nordic countries. It occupies the eastern and southern part of the Scandinavian Peninsula and is a very long country with high mountains in the west. This means that the climate ranges greatly, from temperate to subarctic conditions.

GEOGRAPHICAL ZONES

Sweden measures 1,500km from north to south. It can be divided loosely into six main regions.

THE FERTILE SOUTH

The southernmost part of Sweden, comprising the provinces of Skåne, Halland and Blekinge, is relatively flat. The soil is generally fertile, and the area has been cultivated for several thousand years. The region is densely populated, with many towns and roads. In several places, huge elongated hills stretch through the landscape.

THE EXTENSIVE FORESTS

North of the southern plains, in the province of Småland, there are large coniferous forests. In the past these forests were very difficult to cross, and so they formed the border between Denmark and Sweden – until 1658, the south of Sweden was a part of Denmark. Today the forest areas are far less dense, but the change in landscape is still clearly visible to anyone driving north by road.

LANDSCAPE FEATURES

0 — 200km
0 — 100 miles

N

Torne Träsk
Kebnekaise 2,111m
Muonioälv
Kalixälven
Arctic Circle
Luleälven
Norwegian Sea
SCANDINAVIAN MOUNTAINS
Lake Storuman
Skellefteälven
Umeälven
Gulf of Bothnia
Indalsälven
Lake Storsjön
FINLAND
Ljusnan
Åland Islands
Klarälven
Dalälven
Lake Hjälmaren
Lake Mälaren
Lake Vänern
Göta älv
Baltic Sea
Skagerrak
Lake Vättern
Emån
Gotland
Kattegat
DENMARK
Lagan
Öland
Falsterbo

THE WEST COAST

Sweden's western coast at the Kattegat (the sea between Sweden and Denmark) is mostly low and rocky. The northern part is dotted with many islands, forming an archipelago – or *skärgård* in Swedish. Farther south, the beaches tend to be sandy or muddy.

THE EAST COAST

Sweden's east coast, at the Baltic Sea and the Gulf of Bothnia, stretches for about 1,250km as the crow flies. It incorporates many different coastal features, from rocky bays to sandy beaches. Some distinctive sights are the *skärgård* islands around and south of Stockholm, and the High Coast north of Sundsvall which is known for its beauty.

THE HIGH MOUNTAINS

The Scandinavian (or Kölen) Mountains in western Sweden trace the border with Norway. In Swedish these mountains are called *fjäll*. They reach to a point of 2,111m at Kebnekaise – Sweden's highest peak. Large areas of this mountain range are treeless because of subarctic conditions.

THE GREAT LAKES

Some of Sweden's largest lakes are found in the center of the country. The biggest is Lake Vänern (covering 5,585km^2), but Vättern, Hjälmaren and Mälaren are also considerable in size. It is in the eastern part of this lakeland area that the capital Stockholm and other major cities are situated. South of the lakes is an important agricultural area.

A GLACIAL LANDSCAPE

The Swedish landscape was formed by a massive ice cover, which in the south disappeared 14,000 years ago and in the north 8,500 years ago. The ice scoured away vast amounts of rock and deposited it as a moraine, which varies in thickness and composition in different parts of the country. This glaciation has left Sweden with a relatively thin cover of soil over the solid rock beneath. Also, the great weight of the ice exerted strong pressure, so when it disappeared, the land began rising. This rising of land continues even today – by up to 8mm a year in some parts of Sweden.

CASE STUDY
FALSTERBO BIRD MIGRATION

Falsterbo is a small peninsula that forms the southwestern point of Sweden. This peninsula is well known for its incredible bird migration in the autumn. Thousands of birds stop off here en route from their breeding grounds in the north to their wintering habitats in southern Europe and Africa. At times there have been records of 1,000 honey buzzards, 14,000 buzzards, tens of thousands of swallows and even 145,000

chaffinches in one day! The peninsula works like a giant funnel, concentrating the birds, because they prefer flying over land for as long as possible. But at this point they have to leave the land in order to cross the sea before they reach Denmark. Every year thousands of birdwatchers visit Falsterbo to watch this bird migration. The money they spend on accommodations and food is of great benefit to the local community.

The best months for watching the Falsterbo bird migration are September and October.

LAPPLAND

Lappland is the northernmost part of Sweden and also the biggest province. It is sparsely populated and becoming more so, because opportunities for making a living there are few. One area of reasonable employment is the tourist industry. Mining is also significant in certain parts of the province, but farming and forestry are losing importance. Even though many initiatives have been taken to promote new jobs in Lappland, this part of Sweden has the highest unemployment rate in the country.

MOUNTAIN SCENERY

The western part of Lappland is a zone of mountains, 100km wide, while in the east is a plateau with swamps and forests. The mountains in some places rise above the timberline (the highest point at which trees can grow), and it is in this area that Sweden's highest mountain, Kebnekaise, is found.

High mountains rise near the border with Norway on Lappland's western side.

The Piteälv (Pite River) and its surroundings represent a typical Lappland landscape.

The peaks are separated by long valleys running from northwest to southeast. Here, melted snow and ice and rain from the mountains form great rivers. These give some of the best opportunities in the country for using the power of running water. Several hydroelectric plants have been built across the rivers, providing even the southern parts of Sweden with electricity (see pages 52–53).

People enjoy the short summer in the streets of Kiruna, Lappland's major town.

LAPPLAND'S CLIMATE

The climate in Lappland is determined by the relatively high altitude and its geographical position far north. In the summertime it can be quite warm – sometimes there are even heat waves – but in the winter it is very cold. In the mountains snow and rain are plentiful, but some of the low-lying areas receive very little precipitation. The mountains shelter these parts from the humid winds coming from the Atlantic Ocean.

A PLACE TO VISIT

Tourism is very important for many people in Lappland. Every year, thousands of visitors arrive to enjoy the vast areas of unspoiled nature, many of which have been declared national parks. The tourists come mainly during summertime, and most like to walk along the extensive mountain paths. Others, particularly foreigners, opt to drive through Lappland in their own cars. All the tourists have to use one road – it runs south–north, connecting scattered towns. There are only a few minor roads that cross this major route. Many tourists, especially young people, use public buses to get from place to place.

CASE STUDY
LINNAEUS – A VOYAGE TO LAPPLAND

In 1732, a 25-year-old student was sent to Lappland by the Royal Society of Sciences in Uppsala (just north of Stockholm). He was called Carolus Linnaeus, known in Sweden as Carl von Linné. Linnaeus had shown so much flair for natural sciences that he was appointed to find out if there were any new commercially exploitable resources in Lappland. At that time, Sweden's balance of trade was very poor and the country needed more income. Linnaeus did not find much of economic interest, but he wrote some excellent descriptions of people and nature in the far north. He was especially interested in plants, and his discoveries on this expedition and further visits to other parts of Sweden were important for his later book *Systema Naturae*. This book presents his ideas of the binominal system – the scientific naming format that is still used for all living things today, and for which Linnaeus became famous worldwide. Linnaeus's visit to Lappland has been called the most important expedition in Sweden. Linnaeus was later made professor at the University of Uppsala. He wrote more than 70 books and 300 scientific papers in total, many of which remain influential today.

THE BALTIC ISLANDS

Sweden has thousands of islands along its coasts. Many of them are so small they are uninhabited. But two islands in the Baltic Sea – Gotland and Öland – are considerably bigger. These islands are very popular travel destinations, mostly visited by Swedes. Their climate is different from the rest of Sweden, featuring more hours of sunshine and less rain than any other part of the country.

GOTLAND

The island of Gotland covers 3,140km^2 and is the largest of Sweden's Baltic islands. It can be reached by ferry from Nynäshamn (south of Stockholm) and Oskarshamn, farther down the east coast. The island's biggest town is Visby, where 22,000 of Gotland's 57,300 inhabitants live. Visby is different from all other Swedish towns – so different that it has been declared a World Heritage site by UNESCO. It is a medieval town still littered with very old stone buildings and narrow streets. Also remaining is the original medieval stone wall around its center, measuring 3,500m in length. Every August a medieval festival attracts thousands of visitors to Visby.

Most tourists go to Gotland to experience the vast beaches, the spectacular natural scenery and the wealth of historic places. More than half of Gotland is covered by forest and other rich plant life, including beautiful wild orchids. Scattered in the landscape there are numerous historic monuments, such as medieval churches and beautifully carved stones from Viking days.

Gotland has always been a farming region, but the agriculture has changed significantly during the last half-century. Formerly cattle and sheep roamed large areas, and many of

LEFT: A view of Visby showing St. Mary's Church and part of the extensive old town wall.

BELOW: The islands of Gotland and Öland are well known for their orchids. The military orchid is one of the most impressive of these.

Öland is scattered with traditional windmills that are maintained for tourists but no longer in use.

them were kept inside during the winter, being fed on hay and foliage from trees. Today this kind of agriculture is too time-consuming. But there is a special breed of sheep raised in Gotland that can stay outside in the winter. This breed, called *gutefår*, produces good wool for clothing. But most farmers in Gotland now grow beets, peas and carrots. These are sold fresh or frozen over much of Sweden.

ÖLAND

The island of Öland, covering 1,300km², has a distinctive long and narrow shape. Since 1972, the island has been connected to the mainland by one of Europe's longest road bridges. This has made it easier for tourists to go to Öland, and visitor numbers have quadrupled. The bridge also carries heavy commuter traffic for the many people who live on Öland and work in the mainland city of Kalmar. Today Öland has 24,800 inhabitants, and around 2 million tourists visit the island every year.

Tourists in the summertime come primarily for Öland's beaches. There are numerous campsites and villages with huts where visitors can stay. On days when the weather is not ideal for the beach, tourists have the option of visiting Stora Alvaret, a unique landscape that covers a large part of central Öland. This area is a kind of very flat steppe with only a few centimeters of topsoil. For this reason, it has never been cultivated and is used only for grazing.

In the springtime, Öland is home to a host of rare birds – including a variety of harriers, waders and geese – so it is visited by many bird-watchers. Other people interested in nature also flock at this time, particularly to admire the amazing orchids that flourish due to the calcareous underlying rock.

This rune stone from Öland was erected in the late tenth century, as a memorial to a Danish Viking who died on the island.

CLIMATE

Sweden's climate varies considerably due to the country's great length south-to-north. There are also noticeable climatic differences between coastal areas and inland regions. Although Sweden is very northerly, it has a temperate climate governed by the warm Gulf Stream that passes west of Norway. But in the mountains of the far north, the climate is so cold that it is classed as subarctic.

Most of Sweden is covered by snow in winter. In the mountains of Lappland, the landscape is white for around 225 days a year, but in the south there is much less snow, and sometimes none at all. The low winter temperatures in the north also mean that the Gulf of Bothnia is frozen for long periods of time during this season.

Annual precipitation differs across Sweden. In some mountain areas, around 2,000mm of rain fall each year, as a result of humid air arriving from the Atlantic Ocean. In Småland in the south, there can be up to 1,200mm of annual rainfall. But the eastern parts of Sweden are much drier, with totals of less than 600mm per year in some places.

In the far north of Sweden, the sun is very low in the winter. But there is light 24 hours a day in the summer – the so-called midnight sun.

TEMPERATURE AND RAINFALL

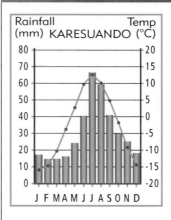

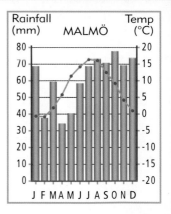

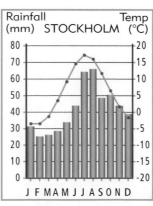

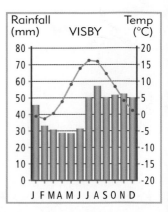

KEY:

Temperature   Rainfall

VEGETATION ZONES

Sweden is traditionally divided into four vegetation zones, based on changes in forest cover.

BIRCH FOREST ZONE

The lower parts of Sweden's western mountains support huge birch forests, with wild herbs and moss growing on the forest floor. In higher-lying places there are shrubs of willow and small bushes including blackberry.

NORTHERN CONIFEROUS ZONE

In the northern coniferous zone, spruce trees dominate, but on drier ground pine, birch, European aspen, rowan and willow also grow. In some areas there are large swamps and bogs with mulberry and plants of the sedge family.

SOUTHERN CONIFEROUS ZONE

The southern coniferous zone is a mixture dominated by conifers, such as pine and spruce, and fewer deciduous trees including oak, ash and elm, but no beech. The forest floor is often covered by blueberry and cowberry, and mosses are also common.

DECIDUOUS FOREST ZONE

Deciduous forest is found in the southernmost parts of Sweden. It consists mainly of beech, but there are also other deciduous trees such as elm and oak. The forest floor is covered with herbs such as dog's mercury and greater stitchwort.

FOREST COVER

- Birch forest
- Northern coniferous
- Southern coniferous
- Deciduous forest

The trees of the birch forests are often scattered and do not grow very high.

Many small forest owners sell their wood for timber or making paper.

Sweden's landscape is rich in natural resources. The extensive forest cover supplies wood that can be used for a variety of different purposes, and mineral-rich rocks offer excellent opportunities for mining.

MINING

There has been mining in Sweden since medieval times. Iron and copper have been the most important metals, but lead, zinc, silver and gold have also been mined in significant amounts. Most of the metals were originally extracted from rocks in central Sweden. Here a vast area became known as Bergslagen, a word that means "the law of the mountains rules."

After the Second World War, there was a huge call for iron for use in rebuilding Europe. So the mines in Bergslagen were modernized to meet demand. In the 1950s, Sweden produced 10 percent of the world's iron ore, and production continued to grow. But competition from other countries meant that all the mines eventually had to close down, and now several of them have been made into museums. In some of these museums you can walk into the buildings where the iron was extracted and see the huge piles of debris outside.

Mines continue to operate in northern Sweden. The biggest is the iron mine in Kiruna, from which iron ore is transported by train to Narvik on the coast of Norway and

MAJOR MINES

Fe	Iron
Cu	Copper
Zn	Zinc
Pb	Lead
Au	Gold
Ag	Silver

The "crater" at the historical Falun copper mine.

The town of Falun in Dalarna grew up because of the copper mine Falu Gruva, or "the Big Copper Mountain" as it is often called. This mine has a long history. Its copper ore has been extracted since medieval times, and in the seventeenth and eighteenth centuries three quarters of all the world's copper came from this single mine. The copper was exported to many countries and produced so much wealth that Sweden in this period became a leading power in Europe. In 1687, some of the galleries collapsed and left a giant crater that now dominates the landscape.

The mine still produces ores, but there is hardly any copper left, so the focus is now on sulfur, zinc and lead.

For several hundred years, some of the excess ore has been made into a special red pigment – Falu red – that is used to paint wooden houses all over Sweden. This pigment is still very popular because it has good protective properties.

Some of the disused galleries at Falun have now been opened to the public, and thousands of people tour the mine with guides. They also visit the museum in the old administration building and nearby workshops. This unique area has been declared a World Heritage site.

shipped abroad to various European countries. The port of Narvik is always free of ice, so iron can be shipped all year. Other mines are Aitik – one of the biggest copper mines in Europe – and Boliden, which still produces economically viable gold, silver and lead. Ore from mines other than Kiruna is taken to the coast of the Baltic Sea, where it is crushed, cleaned and made into pellets for easier transport. Most is exported from here by ship.

PRIVATE FORESTS

In the Swedish countryside, many people have their own forests. Sometimes these are just small woods, but they are big enough to supply the owners with firewood all year round. Often the wood cannot be sold for manufacturing purposes because of low quality, but it is suitable for burning. So people can save a lot of money by heating their houses using wood instead of buying oil.

POPULATION

People relax on the canal-side steps of the highly populated city of Malmö.

POPULATION DENSITY

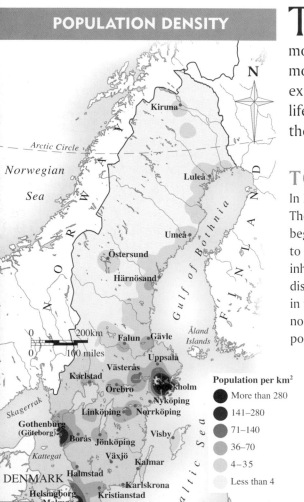

N

Kiruna

Arctic Circle

Norwegian
Sea

Luleå

Umeå

Östersund

Härnösand

Gulf of Bothnia

FINLAND

Åland
Islands

0   200km
0   100 miles

Falun   Gävle
Uppsala
Västerås
Karlstad
Örebro   Stockholm
Nyköping
Linköping   Norrköping

Skagerrak
Gothenburg
(Göteborg)
Borås   Jönköping
Kattegat   Växjö
Kalmar
Halmstad
DENMARK
Helsingborg   Kristianstad
Malmoe
(Malmö)   Trelleborg

Visby

Baltic Sea

Population per km²
- More than 280
- 141–280
- 71–140
- 36–70
- 4–35
- Less than 4

The population of Sweden has risen by 500 percent during the last 300 years. As in most other industrialized countries, the infant mortality rate has become very low and life expectancy is high. Swedes have the highest life expectancy among the Nordic people, and the population's average age is still rising.

TODAY'S POPULATION

In 2004, there were 9,002,500 people living in Sweden. There has been a steady rise in population since the beginning of the twenty-first century, but it is expected to fall again. The average population density is 20 inhabitants per square kilometer, though the distribution of people is very uneven. Most people live in the south and center of the country, while the northern part – especially inland – is very sparsely populated. This affects activities such as industry and trade, which are concentrated around Lake Mälaren (the Stockholm region), around Gothenburg (or Göteborg), and in the Öresund region around the city of Malmö. But there are also population concentrations in parts of Skåne outside the Malmö area, and around Lake Siljan in central Sweden. It is estimated that half the population lives on only 3 percent of Sweden's land.

URBANIZATION

In the last half of the twentieth century, many people in Sweden moved away from rural regions to the bigger towns and cities. This left the sparsely populated areas with further problems. Many local shops, such as grocers, had to close down because they did not have enough customers, forcing the remaining inhabitants to travel long distances to buy essentials such as food. The government has tried to combat this development by giving economic and other kinds of support to these remote areas.

POPULATION STRUCTURE

More boys than girls are born in Sweden, and there are more men than women up to the age of 63. From this age there are more women, because on average women have a longer life expectancy than men. This could be due to a number of factors related to work, general lifestyle and attitudes to health.

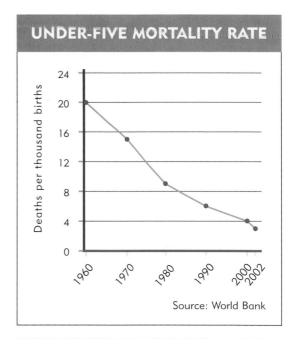

UNDER-FIVE MORTALITY RATE

Deaths per thousand births (y-axis: 0, 4, 8, 12, 16, 20, 24)
(x-axis: 1960, 1970, 1980, 1990, 2000, 2002)

Source: World Bank

Sweden has more elderly women than elderly men. People are living longer as lifestyles become healthier and medical care improves.

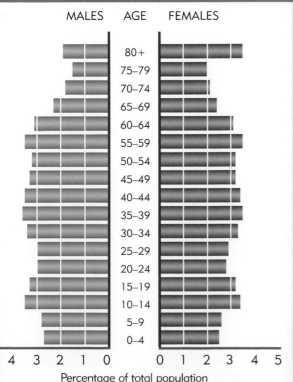

POPULATION STRUCTURE, 2004

MALES	AGE	FEMALES
	80+	
	75–79	
	70–74	
	65–69	
	60–64	
	55–59	
	50–54	
	45–49	
	40–44	
	35–39	
	30–34	
	25–29	
	20–24	
	15–19	
	10–14	
	5–9	
	0–4	

4 3 2 1 0   0 1 2 3 4 5

Percentage of total population

Source: US Census Bureau

EVERYDAY LIFE

The Swedes are a well-off nation with a high standard of living. Most people can afford to buy things they want and spend money on vacations and other leisure activities. Compared with many other Europeans, their outlook is relaxed. Stopping to chat with friends, taking time in a supermarket line and enjoying leisurely strolls are all typical aspects of the Swedish lifestyle.

WORKING ADULTS

Employed people work an average five days a week, normally with Saturdays and Sundays off. Some workers, for example retail staff, have to be more flexible – but 40 hours a week is the maximum anyone needs to put in. Everyone in the labor force is entitled to five weeks' annual vacation.

In the last part of the twentieth century, more and more women took on jobs instead of staying at home to do the housework and look after the children. Women now make up nearly half of Sweden's workforce, and 78 percent of all women of employment age have a job. But they are still paid lower wages than men, despite a Swedish law that states that all men and women should be treated equally.

Boating at Mollösund in western Sweden. Many Swedes have boats for fishing, to travel to their vacation homes or just for fun in their free time.

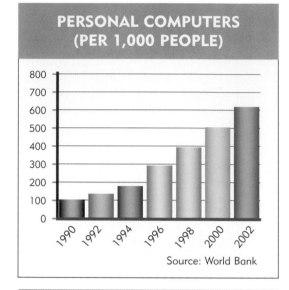

PERSONAL COMPUTERS (PER 1,000 PEOPLE)

Source: World Bank

FEMALE LABOR FORCE (% OF TOTAL)

Source: Social Watch, April 2004

TELEVISION SETS (PER 1,000 PEOPLE)

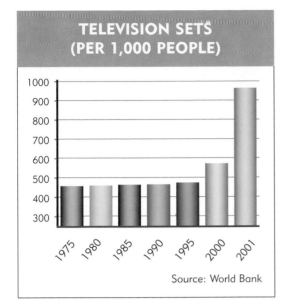

Source: World Bank

provided due to the long distances involved. All students are given a hot lunch at school. Following afternoon classes, many children go on to a club where they enjoy sports, music and other activities while their parents are still at work. Afterward they usually have homework to do. An increasing number of children now have their own televisions, so they can watch their favorite programs when their work is done.

SCHOOLCHILDREN

In Sweden's cities and towns, most children travel to school by bicycle or by bus. In rural areas special school transportation is often

EVERYDAY SHOPPING

Supermarkets in Sweden are often found in the outskirts of a town, in malls where there are also other stores such as sports outfitters and electrical stores. Swedish supermarkets keep longer hours than similar stores in most other European countries – some stay open until late in the evening, almost every day of the year. Because of the long distances many people have to travel for shopping, mail order is also very common in Sweden.

CASE STUDY
SYSTEMBOLAGET

In Sweden it is not possible to buy liquor, wine or strong beer in supermarkets or ordinary stores. Instead, people have to go to special government stores called *Systembolaget*. These are located in every town and city, but in some sparsely populated areas people have to travel a long way to buy alcohol.

The shops get their alcohol from a government-owned monopoly, which is said to have the biggest selection of spirits, wine and beer in the world. But it is the manager of the individual shop who decides what should be available to local customers.

Systembolaget was started in 1850, because some farmers wanted the income from alcohol to benefit the local community and not to be a private profit. Some of these ideas are still in operation, and there are other social advantages. Systembolaget is trying to limit people's alcohol consumption and tell them about the dangers of drinking too much.

Systembolaget shop displays are unenticing, so as not to tempt people to buy alcohol.

Many Swedes own musical instruments and enjoy playing traditional music, or *folkmusik* as they call it. These accordion players are performing at a harvest festival.

TRADITIONS

The Swedes preserve their national customs well. Traditional folk music and folk dance are very popular and are often performed at social gatherings and celebrations. Important instruments in traditional Swedish music are violins and accordions – and there is also a stringed instrument, called the *nyckelharpa*, that is found only in Sweden.

MIDSOMMERFEST

Midsommerfest is the festival of Midsummer, celebrated yearly on the Saturday nearest June 24. It is one of the biggest celebrations in Sweden, and almost everyone takes part. People in many parts of the country dance around a tall pole that has been decorated with leaves and flowers. Originally this tradition was German, but the Swedes have taken it to their heart so much that it is now considered typically Swedish. After the dance,

The decorated pole from the Midsommerfest is left standing to remind people of summer, even when the flowers and leaves have wilted.

people eat, drink and have fun, sometimes late into the night. The decorative pole may be left standing for the rest of the year.

SANTA LUCIA

The Lucia procession is a Swedish custom that takes place just before Christmas. A young girl called the "Lucia bride" leads a parade, wearing a garland decorated with candles on her head. She is followed by other young girls wearing garlands, and they all sing a song about the Christian figure Saint Lucia. The

tradition originated in southern Sweden, but in 1927 a Stockholm newspaper arranged for a Lucia procession to take place in the capital. It soon became widely known and practiced, and has now spread even to other countries. Santa Lucia processions are popular in many hospitals and homes for the elderly.

EATING TRADITIONS

Traditional Swedish cooking has a distinctive style. Many of the national dishes come from the rural kitchen, and they can be very heavy. Salted meats served with potatoes and gravy, and different kinds of porridge, are typical examples. There are also some specialities that the Swedes consider real delicacies.

Every year on the second Wednesday in August, the crayfish season begins. Families and friends gather to eat fresh crayfish along with bread, cheese, beer and schnapps. The crayfish are caught in freshwater ponds and boiled. They are so popular and expensive that in some places people make their own artificial crayfish ponds to ensure they have enough for themselves and their relatives.

Also every year, on the second Thursday of August, northern Sweden launches the season of *surströmning*. People eat small herrings that have been caught in the Baltic Sea and stored in saltwater. After some time, the fish start to ferment and develop a very peculiar flavor and smell – some people even say they are rotten! But the fans of this tradition are not put off by the unusual taste. The herrings are served with flatbread, raw onions and potatoes. This used to be an everyday meal among Swedish peasants.

CASE STUDY
KNÄCKEBRÖD, A SWEDISH SNACK

Knäckebröd is a very crisp, dry type of cracker-bread that is usually made from rye flour, but sometimes also from wheat. It is considered typically Swedish, even though it is also made in other European countries. Baking *knäckebröd* has been a popular tradition for centuries, largely because the bread keeps well for long periods without getting moldy. Today *knäckebröd* is baked in large factories, especially in Dalarna in central Sweden. Most of the bread is eaten in Sweden, but it is also exported to other countries.

Knäckebröd is often eaten as a snack, for example at bedtime. Many people put cheese on it and garnish it with salad; some spread it with marmalade or other toppings. *Knäckebröd* is popular for breakfast, particularly for those on diets.

Knäckebröd served with cheese and salad is a popular snack in Sweden.

IMMIGRATION

There were migrants traveling from Finland to Sweden at the beginning of the nineteenth century. But Sweden's highest immigration figures have occurred since the Second World War. Large numbers still come from Finland, and now around 300,000 Finns live as residents in Sweden.

Like many other European countries, Sweden also receives many immigrants and refugees from Bosnia, the former Yugoslavia and the Middle East. Sweden's immigration policy means it is more open to foreigners than many other countries. This explains why Sweden welcomed a relatively high number of Chilean refugees who fled from the cruel dictatorship of General Pinochet in the 1970s.

Apartment buildings in a Stockholm suburb populated with foreigners. The satellite dishes give residents the option of watching television shows from their home countries.

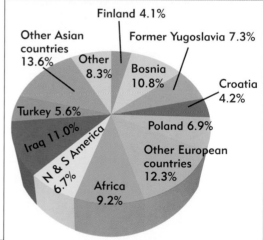

ORIGINS OF IMMIGRANTS, 2002

- Finland 4.1%
- Former Yugoslavia 7.3%
- Other Asian countries 13.6%
- Other 8.3%
- Bosnia 10.8%
- Croatia 4.2%
- Turkey 5.6%
- Poland 6.9%
- Iraq 11.0%
- N & S America 6.7%
- Other European countries 12.3%
- Africa 9.2%

Source: *Statistical Yearbook of Sweden, 2004*

Many immigrants in Swedish towns maintain their own traditions and manner of dress.

Recently, many Danes have migrated to southern Sweden because it is easier and cheaper to get housing there than in Denmark, and because taxes are lower. Around 15 percent of Sweden's current population are of foreign extraction (people who now hold Swedish passports but came from elsewhere, and people who are citizens of other countries). The majority live in the cities.

EMIGRATION

During the nineteenth century, the population of Sweden grew very rapidly and doubled in size. Vast areas of forest were cleared for cultivation, but the increase in crops was still not sufficient to support the many inhabitants. In the middle of the century, Swedes began emigrating, especially to the United States. In some years in the 1860s, more than 1 percent of the Swedish population moved away, creating some of the biggest-ever emigrations from a European country. Emigration was greatest in the 1880s but did not end until about 1930. Some areas in Sweden were heavily affected by this massive loss of population. Many farms were given up and houses and fields abandoned forever.

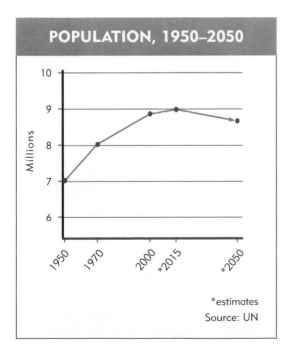

POPULATION, 1950–2050

*estimates
Source: UN

In some areas, such as the province of Småland, the population density fell considerably, making life very tough for people such as grocers and blacksmiths who relied on locals for their trade.

CASE STUDY
THE SWEDES IN AMERICA

The many Swedes emigrating to America in the nineteenth century faced a hard journey by ship across the Atlantic Ocean. Most arrived in New York, where they were registered as immigrants. From here they had to travel farther, primarily to Minnesota and Chicago. The popular belief is that most Swedes settled in the countryside, because they were farmers. But the facts are different. In 1910, 61 percent of Swedish immigrants lived in America's cities. Around this time there were more first- and second-generation Swedes living in Chicago than in Sweden's second-largest city, Gothenburg! For many years the Swedes continued to speak their native language, and they also had their own churches and newspapers.

Today the Swedes are assimilated into American society. However, many still hold on to their heritage. There are currently more than 300 Swedish organizations across the United States, many of which plan events related to Swedish culture. An umbrella organization, The Swedish Council of America, brings together organizations from different states to promote the knowledge of Swedish heritage in America. The organization also works to strengthen cultural and professional ties between the United States and Sweden.

INDIGENOUS POPULATIONS

Beside the Swedes, there are two other indigenous populations in Sweden. These are the Sami and the Finns. There are no tensions between these ethnic groups, and most people's daily lifestyles are similar, whether they are Swedes, Sami or Finns.

THE FINNS

In 1809, Sweden lost most of Finland to Russia. But an area west of the Torne River remained Swedish, and the 50,000 Finnish-speaking people there have since lived in Sweden. Further immigration has made Finns the biggest ethnic minority in Sweden, composing more than 3 percent of the population. In some communities the Finnish and Swedish languages are both officially used, and Finnish radio programs are broadcast in Sweden every day.

THE SAMI

The Sami people live from the Kola Peninsula in Russia through the north of Finland and Sweden to the northern coast of Norway. In Sweden there are Sami as far south as Dalarna in the center of the country. The Sami were formerly called Lapps, but they prefer not to use this name because the word *Lapp* means "patch," referring to the patched clothes that poor Sami wore in the past.

There are 17,000 Sami in Sweden, mostly living in Lappland. They speak their own language as well as Swedish, and in some areas the two languages have the same official status. The Sami were originally reindeer herders, but today most have adjusted to the modern community. The 2,500 or so Sami who still breed reindeer now use helicopters and snowmobiles to follow their herds. Formerly they were nomadic people, moving from place to place in search of grazing and living in *kåte* (huts made from wood, bark and soil) or in summertime tents. With modern transportation this is no longer necessary, so most Sami live in permanent housing instead.

Swedish law states that anyone of Sami origin can own reindeer and allow them to roam free and graze in the wild, but today only a few Sami exercise this right. Reindeer breeders are allowed to let their animals eat mainly lichens in certain unfenced areas.

The Sami are known for their traditional colorful clothes and beautiful handicrafts. Today the traditional clothes are used only for special events such as weddings, but many Sami still craft goods including wood carvings and beaded items. These have become popular tourist souvenirs.

BELOW: The Sami sell traditional handicrafts and reindeer antlers to tourists. This gives them a good supplementary income.

BELOW, RIGHT: The traditional Sami house (*kåte*) was built of wood and turf.

On April 26th 1986, the nuclear plant in Chernobyl in the former Soviet Union exploded. Large amounts of radioactive materials were released and carried by winds to other countries. Among the areas most heavily polluted was the northern Scandinavian Peninsula. Here, the radioactive materials were absorbed by lichens – plants that obtain all their nutrients from the air. Lichens are the main food of the Sami's reindeer, and as a result these animals were also contaminated with radioactivity. When the reindeer were brought to the slaughterhouses the following summer, such high levels of radiation were registered that the slaughterhouses were closed. Some Sami people lost a lot of money, but fortunately not all reindeer herds were affected. For several years reindeer herding had to be given up in some of the worst-hit areas – however, today the problem has almost disappeared.

Reindeer in Sweden are all domesticated, but they are allowed to roam free. Every autumn many are slaughtered for consumption.

THE SWEDISH COMMUNITY MODEL

Sweden is a welfare state, meaning the government is responsible for providing health and social services for all. The Swedish model for community development was widely seen as ideal in the 1970s. Now conditions have changed, partly due to unemployment and immigration. But Sweden is still a country where most people have a relatively high income and social security is strong. Swedes pay many taxes to cover their social services and pension, but taxes are not levied equally on all products and services. For example, food is taxed less than most other things because it is an essential rather than a luxury.

EDUCATION

Swedish children start at preschool when they are six years old. After one year in preschool they have to go to school for nine years. Many young people continue their education with three years in high school. Some subjects are compulsory, but there are also optional courses such as economics/trade, industrial technology, nature/the environment and social studies/politics. All the tuition is free and students can apply for grants if needed, for example to cover the costs of long-distance travel. High school graduates may choose to continue their studies at a university. Most college courses have three levels – a basic education (two years), a further education (three years) and a scientific education (four years). Again, tuition is free, with additional financial support available. So all Swedes have equal opportunities in education.

The Swedish unemployment rate is growing, and many unemployed people can be seen in the city streets.

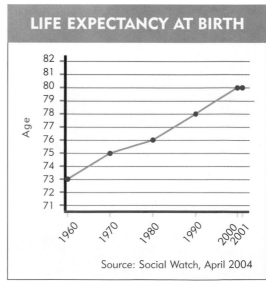

GNI PER CAPITA (US$)

Source: World Bank

LIFE EXPECTANCY AT BIRTH

Source: Social Watch, April 2004

SOCIAL CONDITIONS

In Sweden everyone has social security insurance, offering compensation for lost income during illness or childbirth, or loss of ability to work. The insurance also compensates workers who lose their jobs. This insurance is paid by employers and amounts to one-third of the employees' wages. The money is put into one pool, and the compensation given to people depends on their needs, rather than on how much they have paid during their lifetime.

Swedes can retire when they are between 60 and 70 years old. They then receive a pension from the government. The later they stop working, the bigger their pension will be. Older and disabled people are offered practical help, either in their own homes or at special nursing homes for elderly or disabled people.

HEALTH CARE

In all Swedish towns and cities there are health centers with doctors, clinics for mothers and children, dentists and mobile nursing facilities. In each county (*län*) there are also a central hospital and several smaller hospitals specializing in different kinds of treatment. The cost of medical care is minimal for everybody. People have to pay a small amount to see a doctor and also toward any medicine they might need. But if they are hospitalized, it is free.

All women who work in Sweden are entitled to maternity leave if they have a baby.

Sweden has a high standard of medical care. Specialized hospitals provide quality treatment for those who need it.

AGRICULTURE AND FORESTRY

Swedish farming is highly mechanized, especially in the south where most cereals are grown.

GROWING SEASONS

Growing season (number of days)

- 80–110
- 111–140
- 141–170
- 171–200
- 201–220

Around 4 percent of Sweden's workforce is employed in the primary sector: in agriculture, forestry and fishing. The most important of these is forestry, because Sweden has better conditions for growing trees than for farming. Commercial fishing is very limited.

FARMING PATTERNS

Only 6 percent (about 2,700,000 hectares) of Sweden's land area is used for agriculture. Nearly all farming is concentrated in two areas of the country – the center (west and south of Stockholm) and the south. In the north there is very little farmland.

There are major differences among Sweden's agricultural regions and their products. The differences are due to soil, amount of light, and climate. For example, the growing period in Skåne is nearly twice as long as that in northern Sweden, where winters are long and dark. So farmers in southern Sweden primarily produce crops such as cereals, and farmers in the north keep cattle for dairy products and meat.

The most important cereals are wheat, barley and oats. More than 5 million tonnes of cereals are produced every year. But sugar beets and potatoes are also important crops.

Many crops have their northern limit in Sweden. This means that small annual changes in temperature and rainfall can influence the crop yield considerably. Formerly cattle grazed mostly in areas with poor soil, or where there were many rocks or trees. Today they are found on more open farmland that is no longer useful for crops and has been turned over to pasture. There are about 2 million cattle in Sweden. Pigs are also important, but they are all kept inside large shelters.

DEVELOPMENT IN FARMING

The average farm in Sweden measures around 40 hectares. This is approximately double the size of the average farm in the European Union (EU). Numerous farms, especially smaller ones, have been closed or merged into bigger units. During the twentieth century, the number of farms fell from 300,000 to 90,000, and the total is still decreasing. Between 2000 and 2003 it dropped by 12 percent, so now there are only about 67,500 farms in Sweden. Most of the recently closing farms are small ones that do not receive financial support from the European Union. Larger farms, especially those that produce milk and beef, are given substantial EU grants to keep them going.

Agriculture in Sweden is a vulnerable industry that is heavily affected by weather

The Swedish mountain cow is a common breed in Sweden. It is well adapted to the cool climate.

conditions, especially heavy rain during the harvest period. In some years, about one-fifth of the cereal crops in certain areas have been left to perish on the fields, because the unusually wet weather has prevented harvesting. Until recently, it was traditional to combine agriculture and forestry so that farmers had an income to fall back on if something went wrong on the farm. Today many farm owners still try to maintain some security by taking on another job as well as farming. This is especially common in central and northern parts of the country.

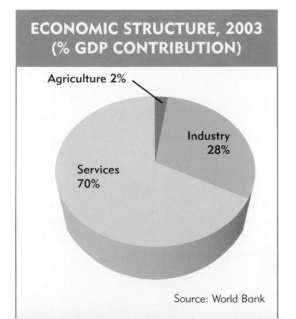

ECONOMIC STRUCTURE, 2003 (% GDP CONTRIBUTION)

Agriculture 2%
Industry 28%
Services 70%

Source: World Bank

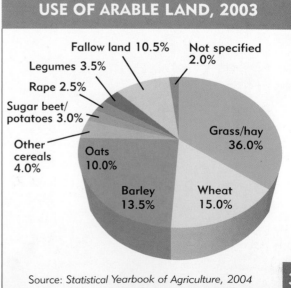

USE OF ARABLE LAND, 2003

Fallow land 10.5%
Legumes 3.5%
Rape 2.5%
Sugar beet/potatoes 3.0%
Other cereals 4.0%
Oats 10.0%
Barley 13.5%
Wheat 15.0%
Grass/hay 36.0%
Not specified 2.0%

Source: *Statistical Yearbook of Agriculture, 2004*

VARIED FORESTS

Forests occupy about 60 percent of Sweden's land area. The various regions look very different because of wide-ranging climatic conditions. In the south, the warmer climate means that trees grow faster and deciduous species dominate. Farther north, conifers take over, and in the mountains birch is most common. But the majority of trees in Swedish forests are conifers, and these are the ones that are generally used to manufacture commercial products such as paper.

FORESTRY

Considering the vast forest area, it is not surprising that forestry has become a major source of income in Sweden. In fact, the country has become the world's fifth-largest exporter of products such as timber and paper – only one third of the produce is used in Sweden itself. Half of the forest area is privately owned, and about one third is owned by companies. The rest belongs to the government.

About 28,000 people work in Sweden's forests. But this number is expected to fall because forestry is becoming more and more mechanized. For example, it is now possible for one person with one machine to cut down a large tree, remove all the branches and saw the trunk into usable pieces in a few minutes.

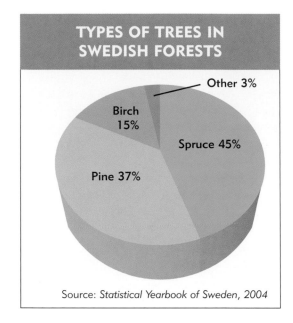

TYPES OF TREES IN SWEDISH FORESTS

Other 3%
Birch 15%
Spruce 45%
Pine 37%

Source: *Statistical Yearbook of Sweden, 2004*

Modern forestry machines cause job losses because they reduce the need for human labor.

PRESERVING THE FORESTS

Every year, about 68 million cubic meters of wood are cut down in Sweden. But this does not mean that the forests are disappearing. When the trees have been cut and sent away, new trees are planted or allowed to grow by themselves. Most forests are replanted, and often this has to be done by hand.

Normally only one tree species is planted or allowed to grow up. This means that the forests risk becoming monocultures with only limited wildlife. But forest managers compensate for this to some extent by planting indigenous tree species to which local wildlife is adapted. Fertilizer and pesticides are used in Swedish forestry, but the amounts of these are falling to a more environmentally friendly level.

Nearly all Swedish forests are used commercially, but there are areas that are protected from logging. Some of these are large national parks, where the primeval trees are virtually untouched by people. Others are smaller areas, such as forests that have been

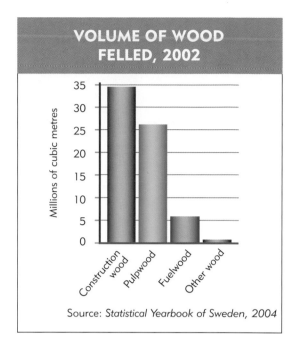

VOLUME OF WOOD FELLED, 2002

Source: *Statistical Yearbook of Sweden, 2004*

grazed by cattle for generations, and these are protected as a combination of natural and cultural heritage. Swampy forests are likewise rarely commercially used.

CASE STUDY
FORESTRY AND THE ENVIRONMENT

According to Swedish law, Sweden's forests are a national resource. They should be managed in such a way that they give sustainable and good yields and at the same time maintain biological diversity. This means that trees and groups of trees should be left as nesting sites for birds, that forest areas along watercourses should be saved, and that specific valuable areas should be

undisturbed. But according to some Swedish NGOs (nongovernmental organizations) this is not always the case. They think that much of the Swedish forestry industry makes too heavy an impact on nature. There are often debates on these issues in magazines, and the NGOs are trying to influence forestry policy as much as possible.

When a forest is logged, groups of trees should always be left behind to support the local wildlife.

TRANSPORTING WOOD

In the past, transporting wood from the forests meant a lot of work. In Sweden this was facilitated by using the rivers. The trees were cut in the wintertime, then pulled to the nearest river by horses. Here they lay waiting for the ice to break, so that they could be floated down the river to a sawmill. Men would balance on the tree trunks while they were floating, to push them so they did not clog. But this system had to change when hydroelectric dams were built across rivers in many places. Now the transportation is done by trucks and trains, and the heavy logs are easily lifted with powerful modern cranes.

MANUFACTURING WOOD

Sawmills today are found in many different places, because energy supplies are so widespread. But originally sawmills lay mainly near rivers, where they utilized the power of the running water. Several of these old sawmills can still be seen in Sweden, but they are now converted to museums.

Traditional log houses in Dalarna make popular vacation homes for people from the big cities.

A VITAL INDUSTRY

The manufacture of wood products is one of Sweden's most important industries. About 74,000 people are involved in making wood or paper products, and no less than 14 percent of Sweden's export earnings comes from these industries.

Sweden produces a lot of processed wood, especially from conifers. Much of this is exported, but a lot of timber is also used within the country – most Swedish houses are built from wood. In recent years Sweden has even started exporting "prefab" wooden houses. The major parts of the houses are manufactured in Sweden, then transported abroad and assembled on the spot. They are ready to move into within just a few days and have a pleasant indoor climate because of the wooden building materials.

PAPER PRODUCTION

Much of the wood from Swedish forests is stripped to its fibers and made into paper. Paper mills are mostly situated along the coasts, and they are often big plants providing many jobs for the local community. But they also cause environmental problems. They use up significant amounts of water in the pulping process, and they release a lot of wastewater containing organic materials that encourage too much algae to grow. Also these industrial plants have a very strong smell, and recently the chemicals used to bleach the paper have been indentified as toxins. Sweden has worked hard to deal with these hazards, and today the country has one of the most environmentally friendly paper industries in the world.

RIGHT: Only a few years ago, paper plants such as this one on the Baltic coast were polluting the sea. Today this is no longer a problem.

The Ikea store in Älmhult, Sweden. Ikea sells furniture and a variety of household items such as mirrors, lamps and towels.

Ikea is a Swedish furniture producer, well known for its modern furniture sold in special warehouse superstores or by mail order. The customers are mainly young families, who love the combination of simple Scandinavian design and low prices, obtained partly because customers have to assemble some of the furniture parts themselves. Ikea was started by Ingvar Kamprad in 1943. He opened his first superstore in Älmhult in Småland in 1958, where Ikea's main plant is still located. Today some 140 furniture superstores are found in about 30 countries around the world. The company started using local Swedish wood and labor, but today Ikea owns forests in, for example, Eastern Europe. More than one third of the production takes place outside Sweden in countries with lower wages.

The end of the production line at the Saab factory in Trollhättan.

Sweden has for many years been renowned for its modern and advanced industry, producing quality items in a distinctive Scandinavian style. The country gained a head start in development, having avoided the devastating setbacks of the two World Wars.

A GREAT COMPETITOR

Sweden's industry is much bigger than that of other Nordic countries – not only because the country is the biggest, but also because its resources, historical conditions and traditions have favored this sector. Swedish companies such as Volvo, Saab, Ericsson and Electrolux are globally renowned. Today around 29 percent of Sweden's workforce is employed in industry.

METAL INDUSTRY

The metal industry is the most important export industry in Sweden, producing about half of the country's export income. Sweden was one of the world's leading producers of iron and steel, so it was natural that it began manufacturing these products, too. Much of the metal industry was established near ironworks in central Sweden, and also in cities elsewhere in the country. One of the best-

MAJOR TRADING PARTNERS (% OF VALUE), 2003

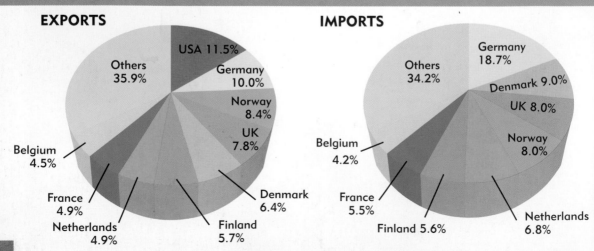

EXPORTS

- Others 35.9%
- USA 11.5%
- Germany 10.0%
- Norway 8.4%
- UK 7.8%
- Denmark 6.4%
- Finland 5.7%
- Netherlands 4.9%
- France 4.9%
- Belgium 4.5%

IMPORTS

- Others 34.2%
- Germany 18.7%
- Denmark 9.0%
- UK 8.0%
- Norway 8.0%
- Netherlands 6.8%
- Finland 5.6%
- France 5.5%
- Belgium 4.2%

Source: *CIA World Factbook, 2004*

known cities, making iron products since the seventeenth century, is Eskilstuna (70km west of Stockholm). Here you can even see some of the original smithies, where hundreds of years ago items such as knives, scissors and tools were made. Today production is much more advanced, and many different goods are made in a mechanized and automated way. As a result of this, and also due to an increase in the use of plastics instead of metal, many jobs in the metal industry have disappeared.

CHEMICALS

Sweden has a very wide-ranging chemicals industry, and many of the products are exported worldwide. Explosives have led the way for many years, invented and set into production by the legendary Alfred Nobel (see case study below). Medicine is another well-known industry, and some of Sweden's medical suppliers, such as Astra, are prominent on the world market. Plastic

This factory makes the famous Swedish "Absolut" vodka from potatoes.

products are becoming more and more important, too – Swedish companies make many quality goods such as household storage boxes that are also popular outside Sweden.

CASE STUDY
ALFRED NOBEL AND THE NOBEL PRIZE

Alfred Nobel (1833–1896) was a Swedish chemist and businessman. In 1865 he invented dynamite, and later he invented explosive gelatin. These and other products made Nobel very wealthy. By the end of his life he owned nearly 100 factories in several different countries.

One year before his death, Nobel decided that some of his money should fund a series of annual awards. He chose to honor leaders in the fields of physics, chemistry, physiology, medicine, literature and peace. In 1969, a Nobel Prize in economics was introduced, funded by

the Swedish National Bank in cooperation with the Nobel Foundation. For reasons that he never explained, Nobel decided that the Peace Prize should be given in Oslo, Norway, which was then in union with Sweden. Nobel Prizes are internationally acclaimed. They are presented every December, mostly in Stockholm, on the anniversary of Nobel's death.

Sweden's royal family attend the Nobel awards ceremony.

ELECTRONICS

Sweden's electronics industry is another strong sector. Telecommunications equipment is in particularly high demand, and the company Ericsson has become a world-leading producer of mobile phones. Most of the production of electronic and electrical equipment is found in the Stockholm area, because this industry needs close contact with other technological companies and research centers. But it is possible to produce advanced electronic equipment in other places, too.

One good example is the camera producer Hasselblad, situated in Gothenburg. For years their cameras have been considered some of the best – in 1969 a Hasselblad camera even became the first camera on the Moon!

VEHICLE MANUFACTURE

Swedish cars are well known for their quality and safety. This has helped to make the relatively small manufacturers big names on the international market. For many years, Volvo in Gothenburg and the smaller Saab in Trollhättan have developed new kinds of safety equipment ahead of much bigger companies in other countries. However, they

Glass workers in Glasriket cut glass after blowing it in liquid form through pipes.

have struggled to compete on a global scale, and today both companies have been taken over by international firms. But Volvo and Saab do not make just cars – they both produce plane engines, too. Saab has also developed advanced military aircraft for many years, and Volvo is well known for its marine engines and construction machines.

Until a few decades ago, Sweden was a major shipbuilding country. But the global market for ships has changed, and competition from shipbuilders in Asia has dramatically reduced production.

TELECOMMUNICATIONS DATA (PER 1,000 PEOPLE)	
Mainline phones	736
Mobile phones	889
Internet users	573
	Source: World Bank

NICHE PRODUCTS AND CRAFTSMANSHIP

A lot of small Swedish industries make specialized products or finely crafted items. These are economically important, nationally and also for export. They include industries making, for example, tents, backpacks and other outdoor equipment, as well as glass items for decorative and household use. In Småland in southern Sweden there is a concentration of 14 glassworks just west of the city of Kalmar. The area is known as *Glasriket*, which means "the Kingdom of Crystal." It is very popular with tourists and produces some of the most famous and artistic glassware in the world.

CASE STUDY
THE DALA HORSE – HANDICRAFT BEING INDUSTRIALIZED

Decorative hand painting is the final step in the making of Dala horses.

In past centuries, Swedish men often spent the long winter evenings in their small houses making toys for children. One of the most popular was a horse cut from wood, and this kind of toy is at least 400 years old in Sweden. From the beginning of the nineteenth century, the horses were also painted. Around Lake Siljan in Dalarna, horses with floral designs became especially popular – so popular that small industries were set up. The horses became known as Dala horses.

In 1939 there was a World Exhibition in New York City. A giant Dala horse was placed outside the Swedish pavilion. The Dala horse became the symbol of Sweden and its fame spread throughout the world. Today, 400,000 horses are manufactured every year, one fifth of them for export. The rough contour of the horse is sawed out industrially, but after that all is handmade. Several people cut the details with a knife, and then the horses are sanded, burnished and painted by hand. So each Dala horse is unique.

The city of Malmö is the commercial center of the south. Shops and services here attract customers from a wide area.

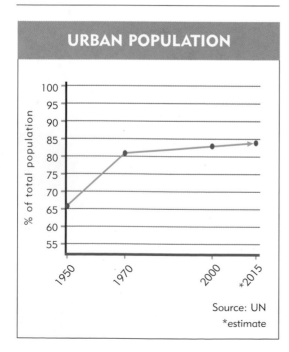

URBAN POPULATION

% of total population

100
95
90
85
80
75
70
65
60
55

1950 1970 2000 *2015

Source: UN
*estimate

SERVICE JOBS

About 4.4 million people in Sweden have a job. No less than 69 percent of these work in services. The Swedish service sector has undergone huge change since the Second World War to support the development of a welfare state. Most service jobs are located in Stockholm and other cities, largely because these places house the major education institutions and commercial centers. Service businesses such as hotels and restaurants are clustered in urban areas, as are cultural venues including concert halls and theaters. Most of these are difficult to move to other places.

But in Sweden the government has supported outlying areas by moving different institutions away from the cities. Also, government offices have been shifted to places where job opportunities are few. For example, the office for paying traffic fines is now situated in Kiruna in the far north.

UNEMPLOYMENT, 1990–2002

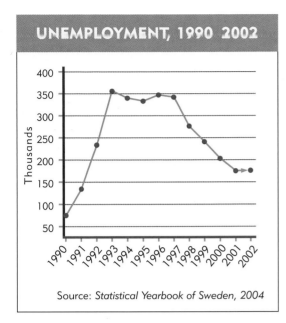

Source: *Statistical Yearbook of Sweden, 2004*

For many years, the Swedish welfare state has maintained that service industries should be run by the government or local councils. But in recent years, which have seen minor crises in the Swedish economy, politicians have been considering privatizing some parts of the public sector. This is a very new way of thinking in Sweden, and it has involved considerable debate. The opponents of privatization fear that the quality of public service will deteriorate if it is sold. But many people think it would be cheaper having private companies providing public service.

SOCIAL AND PERSONAL SERVICES

More than half of the people working in the service sector are employed in social services or personal services. These include nurses and other health care professionals, teachers, office clerks, police, librarians and many others. About 14 percent of service sector employees work in commerce – for example, in stores, bars, hotels or restaurants. Banks and insurance companies employ about 9 percent of the total service workforce. Jobs in the transportation and communication service industries, such as television and radio, account for more than 7 percent.

CASE STUDY
SCIENCE IN THE FAR NORTH

Sweden has for some years been one of the leading nations in space physics. The government has established an institute that carries out basic research, education and observations in space physics, space technology and atmospheric physics. There are four departments in different parts of the country, but the main office is in Kiruna. It was located there to create work and to attract students to this remote town, where other possiblities for making a living are limited. At the institute in Kiruna scientists are developing instruments for satellites and other space equipment. But research into the Earth's atmosphere is also carried out.

The Institute of Space Physics in Kiruna is an independent research center but has links with universities in Umeå and Luleå.

A kayaker sits by her tent on one of the *skärgård* islands.

The Swedes enjoy being in close contact with nature. This means that many leisure activities are connected with the outdoors. In particular, mountain activities such as walking and skiing play an important role in the Swedish lifestyle.

SUMMER LEISURE

Summer activities for Swedish vacationers often involve walking in the mountains of Lappland. Here there are many footpaths, well kept but still in a condition that makes you feel you are walking in the wilderness. The best-known path is the 425km "Royal Trail" (Kungsleden). This was planned more than 100 years ago to make Lappland's mountains accessible for tourists. Located a day's walk apart from each other are various mountain stations, where people can eat and sleep for a reasonable price. Those who don't want to stay at these stations can pitch their own tents almost anywhere.

There are 700,000 houses used for leisure in Sweden, and one in every five families owns a boat. So most Swedes make the most of outdoor life. Many people go sailing around the *skärgård* islands, not only during their long holidays but also at weekends. The thousands of islands in the archipelagos mean that every visit brings a new experience.

WINTER SPORTS

Sweden's most popular winter sport is skiing. Most parts of the country are covered with snow in the wintertime, so skiing has been

a daily form of transportation and leisure activity for centuries. Children often learn to ski at an early age and many come to love it. This also means that Sweden has had several skiers among the world elite. Most Swedish skiing is cross-country, but downhill is becoming increasingly popular.

Ice hockey is another national sport, and Sweden has won the World Championship and the Winter Olympics several times. In recent years, long-distance ice skating on the frozen lakes has flourished, too.

SWEDES ABROAD

Swedes love to travel abroad on charter vacations, particularly to the Mediterranean. Most go during the summer when they traditionally have time off. But many also want to escape the dark Swedish winters and enjoy some long days of sunshine. So Swedes often take vacations abroad more than once a year. It is also common for them to make day trips to Denmark, buying beer, wine and spirits that are not sold as freely in their own country.

BELOW: Cross-country skiing is a widely practiced winter sport among the Swedes.

The Swedish word *allemansrätten* means "the right of public access." It gives people permission to roam and camp in all public and privately owned areas. Anyone is allowed to walk, ski, or ride a bicycle or a horse in all places except near houses and in cultivated areas. There are also some restrictions in nature reserves, but in most areas it is permitted to camp with a tent or RV for one or two nights and to make a fire. Furthermore, *allemansrätten* allows people to collect wild berries and mushrooms and to sail with most kinds of boats on lakes and watercourses. This right of access to nature has been very important in the development of a thriving outdoor lifestyle in Sweden.

Walking in the countryside is one of the most popular outdoor activities in Sweden.

FOREIGN VISITORS

Every year, 14 million foreign visitors come to Sweden. Many of these are businesspeople who spend considerable amounts of money in the country. In 2002, the tourist trade was worth approximately $27 million and gave work to 130,000 people. That is about 2.6 percent of Sweden's gross national income (GNI) – even more than the foreign income from Sweden's car production.

But for the last few years, tourism's share of the gross national income has been stagnating. Tourism is something that the Swedes expect to be more important in the future, because the country's potential has only been partly realized up to now. For example, Sweden is now trying to compete with Norway as an international skiing destination, and fishing is also being promoted to attract foreigners. But the main potential probably lies in the mountains in the northwest of the country. Walking in these vast and desolate areas holds great appeal to other Europeans from more heavily populated areas.

Many day-trippers visit Sweden for special purposes. These are mainly Norwegians and Danes, who come to buy things that are cheaper than in their home countries, such as food, outdoor equipment and car parts.

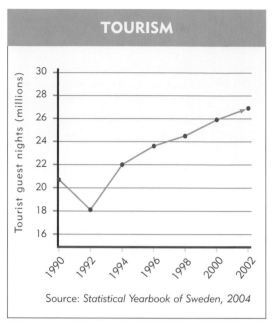

TOURISM

Tourist guest nights (millions)

Source: *Statistical Yearbook of Sweden, 2004*

ÖDEGÅRDE

Many houses in the Swedish countryside have been abandoned because their owners have moved away to towns and cities. These buildings are known as *ödegårde*, meaning "left farm." Some are still kept as vacation homes,

In southern Sweden, many houses left by their owners are sold to foreigners. This ensures that the homes are still maintained.

but many people who want to sell them find it hard to do so. In the southern part of Sweden, however, selling such houses has been possible for many years and seems to be even easier now. Danes, especially those living in the Copenhagen area, seek affordable vacation homes. These are rarely available in Denmark, but in Sweden there is a good market. Thousands of Danes have bought *ödegårde* houses, and now the Germans are also taking an interest. As a result, prices are rising and the better houses are sold very quickly.

Skansen is an open-air museum and zoo in Stockholm, very popular with tourists. The zoo houses a variety of Scandinavian species, including Sweden's national animal, the elk.

CASE STUDY
STOCKHOLM – A CAPITAL TOURIST ATTRACTION

Most tourists visiting Sweden go to enjoy the countryside. But increasingly foreigners are also taking breaks to the capital. Recently, big passenger cruise ships have been allowed to go farther into the *skärgård* to moor at Stockholm, which has helped the cruise industry. Most tourists go to the capital in the summertime, when they can enjoy walking through Gamla Stan, the oldest part of the city. This is a pedestrian area and a very popular place for shopping and eating. Some people think that the original atmosphere has disappeared. But tourist development has also meant many new jobs in the service sector.

The Royal Castle is situated near Gamla Stan. This is the king's workplace, but people can visit it all year round and also watch the spectacular changing of the guard outside. Stockholm is often called "the Venice of the North," because there are so many canals in the city center. Crossing some of the bridges over these canals, tourists can visit other attractions such as museums. One of the most impressive places is the museum of the ship *Vasa* (see page 11).

Thousands of tourists visit Gamla Stan, the old center of Stockholm, with its narrow streets and lanes.

TRANSPORTATION AND ENERGY

Traffic is often very light on the roads in the far north of Sweden.

Until about 150 years ago, river transportation was very important in Sweden. Then railroads were built and trains took over most of the traffic. Later the railways were superseded by roads.

ROADS

Transportation in Sweden today is dominated by road vehicles. Families often have two or more cars, and big trucks transport freight. The roads are generally in excellent condition, but in many places, especially minor routes in the north, they are unpaved. Some of the main roads are now four-lane highways. The speed limit in towns and cities is generally 50km/h, while on countryside roads you are normally allowed to travel at 90km/h. In the far north, where traffic is scarce, the limit is 110km/h, the same as on highways. To fit into continental European conditions, Sweden changed from left-lane driving to right-lane driving in 1967.

RAIL

In the 1850s, the Swedish parliament decided to build a network of railroads. These were placed on separate routes from roads and canals to avoid competition with other traffic. Most, as a result, were built inland. One of the main reasons for building railroads was to develop certain areas such as Lappland. The old rail link Inlandsbanen, connecting central Sweden and the far north, still works – but today it is only a tourist attraction.

Trains were a major mode of transportation in Sweden right up to 1937, but from then on the road system gradually took over, and many rail lines were closed. The government is now trying to encourage people to use railroads for long-distance travel by running very fast and modern trains. The goal is to reduce the amount of fuel-consuming air traffic. Now there are fast trains between Stockholm and cities such as Gothenburg and the Danish capital Copenhagen. These X2000 trains normally run at about 200km/h and have become a real alternative to air travel.

LEFT: This elk warning sign is very common all over Sweden. Every year serious accidents occur when cars collide with large elks.

AIR

The long distances across Sweden are most easily covered by air. There are several airports around the country – Stockholm and Gothenburg have the most international traffic, with regular connections to many countries. The biggest airline is Scandinavian Airlines System (SAS), which is co-owned by the governments of Sweden, Norway and Denmark. The main office of SAS is in Stockholm, even though the main traffic center is Copenhagen. SAS and its related companies dominate most regular air traffic in Sweden and the other Nordic countries.

FERRIES

Many ferries connect Sweden with Germany, Denmark, Finland, the Baltic States and Poland. These are used extensively, not only by passenger vehicles and tourists, but also by trucks carrying export and import products. Fresh fruit and vegetables, for example, are often trucked in from countries such as Holland and Spain – and many industrial products from Sweden are transported abroad in the same way.

A lock raises and lowers boats sailing down the formerly important Göta Canal in central Sweden. Today this waterway is used mainly by yachts.

The Öresundsforbindelsen road-rail connection stretches for 16km between Sweden and Denmark, linking the cities of Malmö and Copenhagen. There are trains at least every half hour, and a steady flow of cars runs all day.

In 2000 Sweden and the European mainland were connected by a combined bridge and a tunnel, called Öresundsforbindelsen (the Öresund Link). Running between the Danish capital, Copenhagen, and the Swedish city of Malmö, it comprises a four-lane highway and also a double-track railway.

One of the ideas behind Öresundsforbindelsen was to make the region around Öresund into a dynamic economic center. Many people now live in Malmö and work in Copenhagen, and vice versa, and cultural links between the two cities are strengthening. However, it will probably be many years before the region is considered a single unit.

ENERGY

Like other modern industrialized nations, Sweden uses a lot of energy. Oil products cost the same as in most other countries, but electricity is comparatively cheap, which means that Swedes use more electricity than most other Europeans. Many people use electric lighting outside their houses all night and leave lights on inside, even when they are away, as a deterrent to burglars.

ENERGY CONSUMPTION

Before oil and electricity were introduced, the Swedes mostly heated their houses with wood fires. Sometimes the wood was converted to charcoal before being used. Poor people also burned peat for warmth. Today oil – and in some areas natural gas – is used for heating. Oil is imported in large quantities (in 2001, imports were an estimated 553,100 barrels per day), and oil accounts for about half of Sweden's energy consumption.

Inevitably, large amounts of energy are also used for transportation. There are many cars in Sweden, and distances within the country are long. As in most European countries, gasoline is expensive because of taxes – but this does not deter the Swedes from driving. Air and noise pollution from cars, however, is only considered a major problem in the cities and along some highways.

Formerly wind energy was used for grinding flour. In some areas, like the island of Öland, windmills were common. But generally there is not enough wind in most parts of Sweden to make wind power a viable resource.

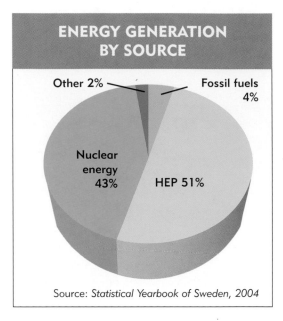

ENERGY GENERATION BY SOURCE

Other 2%

Fossil fuels 4%

Nuclear energy 43%

HEP 51%

Source: *Statistical Yearbook of Sweden, 2004*

HYDROELECTRIC POWER

Hydroelectric power (HEP) is an important source of energy. At the beginning of the twentieth century, many dams and HEP plants were built across rivers in southern Sweden in order to supply the most populated areas with electricity. Many of these are still working, but the pattern has changed. Today it is possible to transport electricity from the far north, where the resources for HEP are strongest,

In many urban areas, homes are heated by hot water running in pipes from heating centers. This creates less air pollution than burning fuel.

to the electricity-consuming areas in the center and south of the country. Sweden also exports large amounts of electricity to neighboring countries such as Denmark. So some very big hydroelectric plants have been built in the river-rich province of Lappland.

Hydroelectricity is normally considered an environmentally friendly and sustainable kind of energy, but the dams that hold the water have damaging effects on the rivers and their animals and plants. For this reason, the Swedes have decided not to use some of the bigger rivers in Lappland for HEP.

NUCLEAR POWER

Sweden has four nuclear power plants. These are situated in the south and center of the country where the demand for electricity is highest. Even though the nuclear plants

This hydroelectric plant in Lappland has been painted with Sami symbols. The plant provides central and southern Sweden with electricity.

produce 43 percent of Sweden's energy, they are not popular among the people. In 1980, a majority of Swedes voted "no" on nuclear power, so some politicians promised to close all plants by 2010. But other politicians were reluctant. As a result, nothing happened and many people were frustrated. In 2005, heavy pressure from the Danes finally led to the closure of the Barsebäck nuclear plant, just 20km from Copenhagen. But nobody knows if this will be followed by the closure of other nuclear sites.

The nuclear plant at Oskarshamn on the Swedish east coast is still in operation.

THE ENVIRONMENT

The wolverine is a protected predator, native to Sweden's northern forests.

Sweden can be considered one of the most environmentally concerned countries in Europe. Because of the Swedes' high education level and affinity with nature, they generally take care of their surroundings. But there is still plenty of work to do in terms of protecting nature and the environment.

NATURE PROTECTION

Sweden has 28 national parks, covering 1.5 percent of the country's area. These are highly protected, but that does not mean people must keep away. Some of the national parks receive thousands of visitors every year. Most are located in mountain areas, but there is even a national park in the suburbs of the capital Stockholm. Weekend walks here are very popular, but despite the number of visitors it is not worn down. This shows the concern most Swedes have for nature.

Sweden's other protected areas are nature reserves – there are 2,400 of them around the country, covering about 10 percent of the landscape. The reserves have been made for many different reasons. Sometimes they form protection for rare species or old trees, but they can also be created to preserve areas that have been heavily influenced by the activities of people and grazing animals. The public has access to nearly all nature reserves.

NATIONAL PARKS

N

Vadvetjåkka
Abisko
Stora Sjöfallet
Padjelanta
Sarek   Muddus
Pieljekaise

Norwegian Sea

NORWAY

FINLAND

Haparanda Skärgård

Björnlandet

Gulf of Bothnia

Skuleskogen

Sånfjället
Töfsingdalen
Hamra
Fulufjället

Åland Islands

Färnebofjärden

Ängsö

Garphyttan
Tresticklan
Djurö   Tyresta
Tiveden

Baltic Sea

Skagerrak

Norra Kvill

Gotska Sandön

Store Mosse

Kattegat

Blå Jungfrun

DENMARK   Söderåsen
Dalby Söderskog
Stenshuvud

0   200km
0   100 miles

CONFLICTS OF INTEREST

In the countryside there is a very strong tradition of hunting. Every year, thousands of Swedes go hunting elk in the autumn. They include people now living in towns and cities who may have family or friends in rural areas. Elk hunting is widely accepted in Sweden, even among the very strong conservationist groups around the country.

Other kinds of hunting are not generally tolerated. The few fishers in Sweden complain that seals and cormorants destroy their fishing tackle, so the Swedish authorities have allowed some hunting of these species to reduce their numbers. But they have also spent the equivalent of millions of dollars on developing fishing equipment that will not be destroyed by the animals and birds. Organizations such as the Swedish Ornithologists' Union have protested against the hunting and there have been big debates – not only among experts, but also among the public whose concern for nature is great.

CASE STUDY
LAKE TÅKERN – AN EXAMPLE OF NATURE MANAGEMENT

Lake Tåkern occupies an area of 45km^2, just east of Lake Vättern in southern Sweden. It is widely considered the most important lake for waterfowl in northern Europe. But it has not been without threat. In 1902, authorities planned to dry out the lake, but protests from nature organizations stopped this. Then in the of mid-twentieth century, farmers reduced their cattle grazing around the lake, letting the grass grow tall. This meant the birds' meadow habitat disappeared and numerous species were threatened. A huge conservation effort resulted. In 1966 the water level was regulated for the benefit of the birds, and the total area became a nature reserve in 1975. Lake Tåkern today is one of Sweden's foremost bird-watching areas, with thousands of visitors every year. The birds can be viewed from a range of watchtowers and hides, and visitors can walk along boardwalks in the wet areas.

A bird-watcher standing on a boardwalk over the wetlands around Lake Tåkern.

A water treatment plant near the town of Trelleborg in southern Sweden.

MONITORING THE ENVIRONMENT

The authorities in Sweden monitor the environment very closely. A special environmental department, directly under the government, works hard to prevent and rectify environmental problems.

WATER MANAGEMENT

Towns and cities in Sweden all have water treatment plants. But in the countryside these are not available. Here, domestic wastewater runs into special filters and is then allowed to percolate into the soil. Because there are so few houses in these areas, this causes no pollution.

A worrysome environmental problem struck Sweden a few decades ago. Water in many of the country's lakes became acidic. Sulfur from the chimneys of industries and houses was being carried through the air, falling on the soil and washing into the lakes. Much of this polluting sulfur came from abroad. The acidic water threatened life in 17,000 lakes, so Sweden took action. Workers started to add lime (calcium oxide) to the lakes to neutralize the acid. This still goes on, but today the pollution has decreased and liming will probably be unnecessary in the near future.

LITTER HANDLING

In nearly all Swedish towns and cities there are so-called environmental stations, where people can get rid of their trash. Everyone is expected to separate their waste – for example colored glass, clear glass, paper and soft plastic – and put it into special containers. These environmental stations are often placed at strategic places such as street corners and supermarkets, and they are used frequently.

Sweden's "environmental stations" do a lot to control pollution in towns and cities.

CASE STUDY
UPPSALA – KEEPING CARS FROM THE CITY

Special double bicycle lanes and parking areas for bicycles are seen all over Uppsala.

Uppsala, 70km to the north of Stockholm, is a university city. This means that large numbers of young people live there and need transportation. Many of Uppsala's residents and students use bicycles, and the city authorities have done much to facilitate bicycle use. Cycle lanes are found throughout the city center and several attempts have been made to reduce the car traffic.

Some years ago, the city tried out a system of electric buses transporting car drivers from parking lots in the outskirts to the city center. The same ticket was used for the parking and the bus ride. Today this park-and-ride system has been abandoned, but people are still discouraged from driving into the city center, now through heavy parking fees and efficient bus services. Some of the buses are powered by biogas and produce less noise and pollution than traditional diesel buses.

Most of the contents are recycled in some way. In addition, household waste is collected from people's homes every week.

RURAL WASTE

For countryside dwellers, garbage handling is not so efficient. People often have to drive a long way to a waste station, and so they don't always take so much care to avoid pollution. Wrecked abandoned cars and farm equipment are often seen littering rural areas.

SWEDEN'S FUTURE

Sweden is running campaigns to combat its environmental problems. But these may be minor issues compared to the challenges the country faces in other fields. Many types of production are migrating to Eastern Europe and the Far East to take advantage of cheap labor in these regions. In order to compete, Sweden needs to specialize its industry. This demands extensive knowledge and a skilled workforce – qualities that the country is developing today.

GLOSSARY

Allemansrätten The special right of public access to all public and privately owned areas in Sweden.

Archipelago A group of islands, or a sea with many islands. In Swedish this is called *skärgård*.

Baltic States The three countries Latvia, Lithuania and Estonia, on the eastern coast of the Baltic Sea.

County (*län*) A large administrative unit in Sweden. A county consists of several municipalities.

Emigration The movement of people away from a country to a new place of residence.

European Union (EU) The group of countries that have joined together to achieve closer political, social, economic and environmental cooperation.

GDP (Gross Domestic Product) The total monetary value of goods and services produced by a country in a single year.

Glaciation The movements and effects of ice masses covering parts of the Earth.

GNI (Gross National Income) The total value of goods and services produced by a country, plus any earnings from overseas, in a single year. It used to be called GNP (Gross National Product).

Gutefår A special breed of sheep from the island of Gotland.

Hydroelectric power (HEP) Electricity generated by water as it passes through turbines.

Immigration The movement of people into a new country of residence.

Indigenous Native to a particular country or area.

Life expectancy The expected lifetime of a person, based on averages and measured in years.

Midnight sun The phenomenon whereby it is light for 24 hours a day during summer months in the far north, with the sun shining even at midnight.

Monoculture Broad cultivation of a single product or species in farming or forestry.

Monopoly Exclusive control over the trading of a particular product or service.

Moraine A mass of debris carried by glaciers and deposited, forming rocky ridges and mounds.

Mortality rate The number of people who die in a year per 1,000 population.

Municipality The smallest administrative unit in Sweden.

Napoleonic Wars The 1792–1815 wars fought between France (led by Napoleon) on one side and several other European countries on the other.

NATO (North Atlantic Treaty Organization) A military alliance formed in 1949 between the United States and several European countries as a means of common protection.

Neutrality Taking no particular side in a dispute or war, and not entering into any fighting.

Peninsula A narrow strip of land pointing out into a sea or lake from the mainland.

Plateau A relatively flat-topped highland.

Population density The number of people living in a particular area, usually counted per square kilometer.

Population structure The numbers and proportion of people in particular age groups within a given population.

Precipitation A general term for rain, hail, snow and the like.

Province (*landskap*) One of the large regions into which Sweden was historically divided.

Refugee A migrant who has been forced to flee from his/her home country, for instance by war.

Scandinavia A region of northern Europe that includes the kingdoms of Sweden, Norway, Denmark, Finland, Iceland, Greenland (belonging to Denmark), the Faroe Islands (also Denmark) and the Åland Islands (belonging to Finland). Also known as the Nordic countries.

Scandinavian Peninsula The landmass in northern Europe that is occupied by Norway and Sweden and separated from Finland by the Gulf of Bothnia.

Steppe An extensive lowland plain dominated by grasses and herbs, usually without trees.

Subarctic Related to regions immediately south of the Arctic Circle. Cold, sometimes severe winters and relatively warm summers are characteristic.

Temperate Having a moderate or mild climate. The world's temperate zones lie between the Arctic Circle and the tropic of Cancer and between the Antarctic Circle and the tropic of Capricorn.

Timberline The highest altitude at which trees can grow and survive.

UNESCO (United Nations Educational, Scientific and Cultural Organization) A UN branch founded in 1945 to promote international cooperation in the fields of education, science, culture and communication.

Welfare state The system of public services that is set up within a country for the benefit of the population, including free medical care, education and free use of libraries.

FURTHER INFORMATION

BOOKS TO READ:

Anderson, Margaret J. *Carl Linnaeus: Father of Classification*. Springfield, N.J.: Enslow Publishers, 1997. A biography of the Swedish naturalist who invented the international system for naming animals and plants.

Gan, Delice, and Leslie Jermyn. *Cultures of the World: Sweden*. 2d ed. New York: Benchmark Books, 2003. A colorfully illustrated survey of the geography, history, economy, and culture of the fourth-largest country in Europe.

Nordstrom, Byron J. *The History of Sweden*. Westport, Conn.: Greenwood Press, 2002. An informative chronicle of Sweden, from Viking times to the country's present-day culture and politics.

Streiffert, Bo, ed. *Eyewitness Travel Guide: Sweden*. New York: Dorling Kindersley, 2005. A guidebook that includes features on Sweden's culture, folklore, and traditions, as well as useful 3D models and maps.

WEBSITES:

The CIA World Factbook
http://cia.gov/cia/publications/factbook/geos/sw.html
The US Central Intelligence Agency's online factbook, with statistics and assessments of all countries of the world.

Statistics Sweden
http://www.scb.se
The Swedish government's official statistics website.

National Atlas of Sweden
http://www.sna.se/webatlas/index.html
Includes maps on a variety of themes.

Visit Sweden
http://www.visit-sweden.com
Website of the Swedish Travel and Tourism Council.

Sweden.se
http://sweden.se
The official website for information about Sweden.

The City of Stockholm
http://www2.stockholm.se/english
The official website of the Swedish capital, Stockholm.

The Swedish Council of America
http://www.swedishcouncil.org
Website of an umbrella organization covering Swedish-American groups and organizations and their activities in the United States and Canada.

METRIC CONVERSION TABLE

To convert	to	do this
mm (millimeters)	inches	divide by 25.4
cm (centimeters)	inches	divide by 2.54
m (meters)	feet	multiply by 3.281
m (meters)	yards	multiply by 1.094
km (kilometers)	yards	multiply by 1094
km (kilometers)	miles	divide by 1.6093
kilometers per hour	miles per hour	divide by 1.6093
cm^2 (square centimeters)	square inches	divide by 6.452
m^2 (square meters)	square feet	multiply by 10.76
m^2 (square meters)	square yards	multiply by 1.196
km^2 (square kilometers)	square miles	divide by 2.59
km^2 (square kilometers)	acres	multiply by 247.1
hectares	acres	multiply by 2.471
cm^3 (cubic centimeters)	cubic inches	multiply by 16.387
m^3 (cubic meters)	cubic yards	multiply by 1.308
l (liters)	pints	multiply by 2.113
l (liters)	gallons	divide by 3.785
g (grams)	ounces	divide by 28.329
kg (kilograms)	pounds	multiply by 2.205
metric tonnes	short tons	multiply by 1.1023
metric tonnes	long tons	multiply by 0.9842
BTUs (British thermal units)	kWh (kilowatt-hours)	divide by 3,415.3
watts	horsepower	multiply by 0.001341
kWh (kilowatt-hours)	horsepower-hours	multiply by 1.341
MW (megawatts)	horsepower	multiply by 1,341
gigawatts per hour	horsepower per hour	multiply by 1,341,000
°C (degrees Celsius)	°F (degrees Fahrenheit)	multiply by 1.8 then add 32

INDEX

Numbers shown in **bold** refer to pages with maps, graphic illustrations or photographs

Young Swedes follow fashion and enjoy a modern lifestyle, whether they live in a city or in the countryside.

The high-speed X2000 trains
run between major cities and
offer strong competition to
air travel.